Corporate Social Responsibility

Self-Assessment Guide

INTRODUCTION 7

How to use this CSR Self-Assessment Guide 7

The best people to undertake the CSR self-assessment 7

The benefits of completing a CSR self-assessment 8

BEFORE UNDERTAKING CSR SELF-ASSESSMENT 9

GOVERNANCE 11

Indicator 1: Does the organization identify its significant economic, social and environmental impacts? 13

Indicator 2: Does the organization have a CSR strategy that defines its commitments to CSR? 17

Indicator 3: Does the organization have designated senior personnel with clear responsibility for CSR?................................19

Indicator 4: Does the organization link corporate responsibility issues to staff performance reviews? 23

Indicator 5: Are CSR priorities defined and communicated throughout the organization?..25

ENVIRONMENT..27

Indicator 6: Does the organization have action plans and programmes to minimize its environmental impacts? 29

Indicator 7: Does the organization maintain a monitoring system, measuring the significant environmental impacts? 33

Indicator 8: Does the organization have a training programme to help employees implement its environmental policy and action plan?..35

Indicator 9: Can the organization show a quantifiable reduction in annual carbon emissions?..37

Indicator 10: Does the organization have a recycling programme?39

LABOR RELATIONS 41

Indicator 11: Does the organization have a regularly evaluated action plan regarding labor and human resources? 43

Indicator 12: Do employees have official representation in the organization? 45

Indicator 13: Does the organization have a health and safety system? 47

Indicator 14: Does the organization have plans to mitigate the adverse impacts of job reductions? 49

Indicator 15: Does the organization have an effective grievance procedure? 51

COMMUNITY RELATIONS...53

Indicator 16: Does the organization have a community engagement action plan? 55

Indicator 17: Does the organization engage in regular dialogue with its key stakeholders? 57

Indicator 18: Does the organization actively participate in CSR associations and forums or engage with any local charities? 61

Indicator 19: Does the organization offer volunteering time, invest in or support any local community initiatives? 63

Indicator 20: Does the organization offer training schemes to facilitate skills development? 65

BUSINESS ENVIRONMENT 67

Indicator 21: Does the organization assess the human rights, health and safety, anti-corruption and environmental practices of its supply chain? 69

Indicator 22: Does the organization engage in sustainable procurement? 73

Indicator 23: Does the organization have anti-bribery and corruption procedures? 75

Indicator 24: Does the organization have a policy and procedure for making its lobbying efforts transparent? 77

Indicator 25: Does the organization train its staff on ethical supply chain measures and anti-bribery and anti-corruption measures? ..79

EXAMPLE ASSESSMENT-SCORING TEMPLATE...............................81

Introduction

This Guide helps organizations both big and small assess their activities and their level of Corporate Social Responsibility compliance. More specifically, this Guide also provides a way for any organization to measure its CSR performance, so enabling comparison over time and against organization and third-party benchmarks.

How to use this CSR Self-Assessment Guide

Using a questionnaire with 25 focused CSR indicators, this CSR Self-Assessment Guide helps users to investigate five key CSR-related areas that are common to most business, i.e.: *Governance, Environment, Labour Relations, Community Relations* and *Business Environment*.

The answers given to this assessment are then analysed and scored by the assessor in a robust, logical and defensible way. For each indicator, the scoring method and scoring criteria are explained to help show assessors how the scoring should work.

The total maximum available score for all the 25 indicators is 100 points. As all categories are equally important for sustainability the 100 points are shared equally between the key CSR-related areas. This then allows responses to be ranked and helps to highlight the significant CSR issues affecting the organization in a prioritised way.

The best people to undertake the CSR self-assessment

To avoid bias and false results, this CSR Self-Assessment should not be done by one person working alone. It is much better to have a small group of people from different departments and organizational levels of the organization to do the assessment together. This will give a broader, much richer and more accurate view of the organization's CSR activities.

The benefits of completing a CSR self-assessment

The benefits of completing this CSR Self-Assessment are:

- Clear, usable outcomes.
- The results of the Assessment bring insights from the organization's internal departments as well as from external sources.
- That unforeseen, but positive, outcomes can be achieved. For example, streamlining policies and connecting CSR responsibilities to board members' remuneration.

The benefits of using this Guide over others are that it allows organizations to:

1. Identify what works well with respect to CSR, and in what areas the organization has achieved (or not achieved) its CSR goals.
2. Better understand the issues that are helping or hindering the organization achieve better CSR performance. Such issues can be manifest within the organization or emanate from outside the organization.
3. Show areas within the business that are operating in harmony with CSR goals and those that are problematic, what obstacles and difficulties exist. It will be easier then to update CSR priorities.

Before undertaking CSR self-assessment

The information that you need will need to complete this assessment will come from different parts of the organization. The person responsible for the assessment should therefore meet with other department representatives to clarify the information needed. To enable more reliable results to be gained it is recommended not to do the self-assessment alone, nor to rely exclusively on your own knowledge or corporate documents.

This is a Self-Assessment Guide which can be useful to identify gaps in the organization's CSR commitments. As such, the organization's evaluator should avoid aiming to give the highest score for the performance if it does not fulfill the criteria or if there is no written evidence for it. Hence try not to focus on the best possible results, but rather evaluate the current situation truthfully – otherwise the Guide would be of little use and would not be suitable for comparison.

Some interpretation of the Self-Assessment questions may be required if procedures, policies, committees, etc. have a different name in your organization. Keep in mind the logic of your organization when you think about the answers. However, note that this should not result in a reinterpretation that totally contradicts the intentions and spirit of the assessment.

Do not be afraid of having low(er) assessment scores. You probably will have at least one category where you perform (relatively) well. You can be pleased that and then try to catch up in other categories.

Do be aware when evaluating yourself and the organization for which you work. There are some inherent risks related to honesty in the information provided. Being the evaluator and the evaluated subject at the same time is sometimes difficult. Self-assessment tools vary in their abilities to avoid such honesty problems. This Guide aims to depict a rather complex issue (CSR) in a fairly simple way (i.e. by posing 25 questions). This may tempt users to falsely view the CSR Self-Assessment Guide as a 'tick box' exercise. There can also be a harmful tendency to provide better-than-real results. This is often done to please powerful stakeholders such as the boss or influential shareholders or to falsely compare more favorably against competitors. Even if such temptations can be avoided, organizational loyalty or ignorance of the facts can also provide false results.

Using the Self-Assessment Guide's logical methodology will allow an overall CSR score to be calculated. This score can provide a useful benchmark: a benchmark not just for the organization over time, but also compared to other similar organizations. Just bear in mind that such comparisons should be done with the knowledge that the rigor of the Self-Assessment and the honesty of inputted data upon which the result is based, will differ amongst organizations.

Governance

Governance in a business context is all about how the organization is controlled and operated and the systems and rules used to do this. Corporate governance therefore is about balancing the needs of stakeholders. The senior management team of the organization are the main influencers on this aspect of the business.

Poor governance can lead to influential stakeholders questioning the levels of trust, reliability and integrity they have in the organization. Therefore, ensuring that the organization is governed properly is critical for success. This is what the first set of 5 indicators focus upon.

CATEGORY: GOVERNANCE

Indicator 1: Does the organization identify its significant economic, social and environmental impacts?

The first step to developing an effective CSR programme is to make sure the organization has defined its social, environmental and economic impact factors. This is the first step in developing a useful CSR strategy.

'Economic impact' (i.e. Profit) means money, wealth e.g. taxes paid, and the value added to society throughout the supply chain.

'Social impact' (i.e. People) means organizations, communities, staff e.g. how the local community benefits from the organization's presence or how its services/products make a positive difference.

'Environmental impact' (i.e. Planet) means the natural world, e.g. water usage and waste production.

Potential sources of information

Any relevant document that includes details about these impact indicators and their impact. The organization's financial information, annual reports, contracts, utility bills, etc.

Practical tips

This indicator may provide a starting point for revision of existing or development of a new CSR strategy. It also may be used for developing a CSR report and assist in creation of a good framework for CSR activities.

Depending on the sector, impacts may be differently distributed (e.g. usually 'environment' has the heaviest weighting although this is dependent upon the organization's context. If in doubt distribute the impacts evenly amongst the three categories: Profit, People and Planet.

International standards ISO14001 and SA8000 ask organizations to analyse impacts and so can provide a starting point for this assessment.

Indirect impacts in some sectors (e.g. financial sector) might have significant society effects. For example, the direct environmental impacts of a bank's offices are usually small (e.g. use and disposal of paper, energy and fuel). The indirect impacts however, resulting perhaps from the bank's credit policy are much more significant. A bank may strongly influence the technology they use by considering the ecological risks. Similarly, with their social impact – some banks are demanding with respect to holding dialog with their local communities, developing new technology and can thus stimulate better industry behaviour.

Methodology

1. Review the organization's financial records to assess strengths and weaknesses.
2. Review the organization's contracts and obligations and assess whether they are being upheld.
3. Review the organization's energy use, water use and waste disposal practices to determine in what ways it is impacting the environment.
4. Determine the scale of each impact.
5. Rank the impacts according to the scale of the impact.

Scoring

Total score available: 4 pts; If answered Yes = 4 pts; Yes, but only partially = 2 pts; No = 0 pts

Organizations should assess their impacts, both positive and negative, with respect to the:

- Nature of business and how the business operates. This should include normal operations, as well as emergency scenarios and abnormal times, such as during holiday periods.
- Product/service life cycle
- Supply chain
- Stakeholders, especially those most powerful and influential.

CATEGORY: GOVERNANCE

- Environment

    Score full points if the organization fulfills this indicator completely, 2 points for partial fulfillment and no points if they fail to map any of the 3 elements i.e. (Profit, People and Planet).

CATEGORY: GOVERNANCE

Indicator 2: Does the organization have a CSR strategy that defines its commitments to CSR?

An organization is considered to have a CSR strategy if it has policies which identify goals, responsibilities and Key Performance Indicators in the following areas: Environmental, Labour, Community Relations and the Business Environment.

For an organization to practice CSR, it needs to have discussed what CSR means for the organization. This process can best happen through development of a CSR policy, which encourages the organization to think about how it will approach CSR and is accounting for CSR at a senior level to ensure the delivery of tangible results.

Potential sources of information

Any types of documents which can consist of one or several separate documents and it can be published externally or simply be internal. Also written strategy, meeting agendas and minutes, notes on discussions that led to the formation of the CSR policy, written evidence of periodic reviews of the policy.

Practical tips

If CSR is not embedded into business strategies, CSR activities often result in fragmented and uncoordinated philanthropic activities, disconnected from, and not helping the, organization's strategy. The strategy should include the main areas of operation and interests of the organization and express the organization's CSR commitments, describe desired objectives and provide a basis for the measurement of outcomes.

Goals and Key Performance Indicators should be developed in each of the categories, i.e. Profit, People and Planet.

Methodology

1. Align the CSR strategy with the organization's needs and culture.
2. Consult with key stakeholders.

3. Ensure then that the CSR strategy gains approval by senior managers.

4. Regularly, i.e. at least annually, assess and revise the strategy

Scoring

Total score available: 4 pts; If answered Yes = 4 pts; Yes, but only partially = 2 pts; No = 0 pts

To obtain 4 points, the policies should cover all aspects of the CSR strategy. 2 points will be given to those organizations covering some but not all of the content. No points if there is no strategy in place at all.

Indicator 3: Does the organization have designated senior personnel with clear responsibility for CSR?

'Senior' means someone who has the authority to make decisions and act on CSR without having to consult more than one person for permission.

'Clear responsibility' means that CSR must be part of this person's job function, although this does not have to be full time.

Just as people are far more likely to implement CSR if they have clear job functions, they are far more likely to act on CSR objectives if a person in authority to consult and provide guidance on CSR practice.

Conversely, if people in authority have oversight of CSR activities, they usually have an understanding and knowledge of the business and can know best how to enact CSR from a practical perspective.

Potential sources of information

Organization charts with CSR roles included within them, CSR roles and responsibilities written into job descriptions.

Practical tips

Some organizations that have a CSR role in existence may find such a role located within, or at least close to, Marketing and Communications departments. If so, that might create potential risk that CSR be focused on communication and brand-enhancing actions only. CSR responsibility is an over-arching function and should be located close to corporate level management. Assigning CSR decision-making to the Management Board safeguards that CSR issues will be managed at an appropriately strategic level.

The criteria of this indicator might be understood more broadly. For instance, if there are no single senior personnel with clear CSR responsibility, but CSR responsibility is included in the job description/task of all board members one can consider that the clear responsibility for and decision-making capability on CSR does exist. Notably, assigning CSR responsibilities to some senior managers ensures that CSR initiatives will receive attention at management level. For example, the following are some possible scenarios:

- a sitting board member could be tasked with the broad responsibility of overseeing CSR activities; or
- a new board member with specific CSR expertise could be appointed; or
- CSR responsibilities could be added to the work of existing board committees; or
- the entire board could be involved in CSR decisions.

Methodology

1. Determine staff CSR responsibilities – these need not be full-time positions.
2. Ensure a senior level employee implements and oversees the organization's CSR programme.
3. Ensure organization-wide engagement of employees.
4. Work with local communities, governments and other key stakeholders to ensure that the CSR job functions encompass all material, social and environmental impacts of the organization.

Scoring

Total score available: 4 pts; Senior staff member with full-time responsibility for CSR = 4 pts; Senior staff member with part-time responsibility for CSR = 2 pts; No senior staff member with responsibility for CSR = 0 pts

At least one person at director level must implement and oversee the organization's CSR objectives. To ensure buy-in, and to propel momentum, it is good if several people have CSR components to their jobs, but there should be one person with overall responsibility. This person needs not have CSR as a sole job function for the organization to receive points under this indicator, but a dedicated senior-level staff member with full CSR responsibility will receive the highest points.

CATEGORY: GOVERNANCE

Indicator 4: Does the organization link corporate responsibility issues to staff performance reviews?

Where relevant, this means that social and environmental issues are actively considered as part of the appraisal process across the organization. For example, if employees fail to deliver on CSR issues, their performance reviews should reflect negatively.

Relevance

People are far more likely to enact CSR goals if the goals are built into their job descriptions and if they are then evaluated on those descriptions and job functions.

Potential sources of information

Key Performance Indicators, statistics reflecting performance on the CSR indicators, employee reviews reflecting evaluations on CSR Performance Indicators, documentation on problems that arise for staff trying to reconcile business related CSR priorities.

Practical tips

Documented information reflecting performance on the CSR indicators and linked to staff performance is important for successful execution of CSR in an organization. Lack of such solutions reflects relatively shallow implementation of CSR philosophy and poor CSR management.

Many Key Performance Indicators will not, on their own, improve CSR performance. It is usually better to select fewer indicators, but ones of greater relevance for achieving the organization's mission. This is then ore likely to create positive change.

To achieve some quick successes, it's usually wise to start with some CSR related Indicators exclusively for CSR related personnel (e.g. the Environmental, HR and Marketing managers), later expanding to all employees.

For example, underlying a commitment to address climate

change by managing its energy consumption and reducing its GHG release, the organization might set a goal to annually reduce its CO_2 emissions. Quarterly targets could then be established which would be monitored and evaluated to track progress. A Key Performance Indicator would be, for example, electricity consumption with the measurement method as recording the kilowatt hours of electricity used each month. A regular review of the commitments, objectives, indicators and measurement methods may lead an organization to modify its CSR objectives. For instance, the organization may finally conclude that in order to achieve the CO_2 emissions target through reduction in energy consumption, all employees need to be aware of the goal and become involved. Thus, an additional target of staff awareness of the organization's commitment to address climate change should then be added.

Methodology

1. Ensure that CSR performance indicators are included in employees' Key Performance Indicators and that they are made aware of this.
2. Ensure that employees are evaluated on CSR indicators in their performance reviews.
3. Ensure that CSR performance indicators are weighted heavily enough in the review to be taken seriously by both managers and employees.

Scoring

Total score available: 4 pts; Yes = 4 pts; Yes, but only partially = 2 pts; No = 0 pts

The organization must uphold business incentives for staff to ensure that good CSR performance is held as an important dimension to the organization's work.

Senior managers must offer support for their staff in determining ways to practice CSR when they have difficulty reconciling business incentives and CSR incentives. So, aligning CSR incentives strongly with business incentives will achieve the highest score for this indicator.

Indicator 5: Are CSR priorities defined and communicated throughout the organization?

This indicator is concerned with ensuring that everyone, not just the senior staff, has clear CSR responsibilities and understands the 'bigger picture'. 'Key CSR priorities' means those responsibilities that make CSR a strategic element of the organization's business.

'Communication' means effectively disseminating an understanding of CSR responsibilities and functions.

Unless people understand that CSR is a part of their job responsibilities and how to fulfill these responsibilities, it is unlikely that they will be able to fulfil their CSR role within the organization.

Allowing people to better understand the broader picture will also embed CSR beyond senior management levels, enabling staff to converse confidently about such issues outside of their workplace.

Potential sources of information

Job descriptions, sign in sheets for organization or departmental meetings when the CSR strategy is discussed, sign in sheets for CSR training and CSR information materials.

Practical tips

Internal communication on CSR usually exists in all organizations that are concerned about this issue. However, the scope might be different in different organizations. For example, more stress being placed upon environmental issues only.

Employees should be encouraged to accept and be enthusiastic about implementing CSR initiatives. This will happen when they believe that senior management is serious about CSR and acts in a manner that reflects the spirit of the commitments.

Internal communication can mean such ways as the intranet, internal magazines, and the organization's Annual CSR Report.

Methodology

1. Ensure that key CSR responsibilities are defined in a CSR policy/strategy.
2. Ensure that the CSR policy/strategy is communicated regularly to staff; this can be through postings in the workplace, through talks and training sessions or through CSR committees.
3. Ensure that employees receive communication about their CSR responsibilities that are relevant to their job function

Scoring

Total score available: 4 pts; There is a mechanism in place to communicate CSR priorities and news regularly, including during introductions for new hires = 4 pts; The organization communicates CSR priorities and expectations to all staff annually = 2 pts; There is no communication of CSR priorities to employees = 0 pts

Key CSR priorities and their business context must be clearly stated in a written document. For example, a CSR policy or CSR strategy.

The organization must make an effort to convey its CSR expectations to both staff with direct CSR responsibilities and those without specific CSR responsibilities (it could well be, for instance, that someone without a direct CSR role has a job function that enables someone with a CSR role to carry out their CSR job).

Therefore, communication about CSR within the organization when CSR decisions are taken, and at the point of hire, will receive the highest score under this indicator.

Environment

The environmental category of this Assessment focuses upon the physical surroundings and natural systems in which the organization exists and its impact upon those systems. Environmental concerns can be very local, such as the effect the organization has upon a nearby river or aquifer. The organization can also affect the environment further afield, such as air-borne pollutants travelling around the planet.

The next 5 indicators within this assessment therefore probe how the organization is affecting the environment and what, if anything, is being done to minimize any potential harm.

CATEGORY: ENVIRONMENT

Indicator 6: Does the organization have action plans and programmes to minimize its environmental impacts?

An Environmental Action Plan should include:

- Improvement goals and targets. These should be linked to environmentally beneficial targets such as minimizing carbon emission and use of energy, water, paper, and other raw materials, as well as boosting rate of recycling.
- Actions necessary to meet targets.
- Defined responsibilities for each action.
- Time limits for actions to be completed.
- Monitoring and evaluation methods.
- How progress about actions is communicated.

An organization could have several environmental impacts and concerns. In order to begin addressing them, the organization needs to prioritize and develop a strategy on how to tackle such issues. This element is considered in Indicator 1.

What follows from determining such impacts is how to fix them. That's where an action plan comes in. It is important that it doesn't just tell people what to fix, but also describes specific goals and actions that need to be taken regarding how to prevent problems reoccurring.

Potential sources of information

Documented environmental policy and environmental performance action plans.

Practical tips

Environmental responsibility is an especially important thing to assess for those organizations that have a major impact on the environment. This could be due to the nature of their production activities or the products and services that they produce and/or rely on natural resources and a buoyant and healthy environment.

Notably, the organizations with limited influence on the environment might score themselves with fewer points. However, they may not perform poorer than colleagues from more 'polluting' sectors. What is important here when doing this assessment, is to ensure that both direct and indirect impacts are considered. For instance, financial and professional services organizations, especially in banking, insurance, fund management, auditing and accounting, and information technology and media organizations, have a crucial influence on promoting more sustainable production and consumption patterns. These include the potential for cost savings, more efficient production processes, product and service innovation, access to new markets, improved risk management, and better stakeholder relations. These are the indirect impacts of their work.

Methodology

1. Meet with senior staff to establish targets for improving environmental performance.
2. Maintain statistics that are relevant to the environmental performance of agreed targets and metrics.
3. Based on the statistical analysis, create an action plan for improving environmental performance.

Use elements of the action plan to demonstrate the change in the levels of the organization's environmental impacts over time and with respect to sector best practice.

Scoring

Replaces 'answer key' + 'criteria'

Total score available: 4 pts; The organization's environmental action plan is comprehensive and includes an evaluation of progress against Key Performance Indicators = 4 pts; The organization's environmental action plan does not include all required components but does include an evaluation of progress against Key Performance Indicators = 2 pts; The organization does not have an environmental action plan = 0 pts

CATEGORY: ENVIRONMENT

The environmental action plan must contain actions that the organization will take to fix problems. Simply stating problems is insufficient. The plan should provide deadlines by which actions should be completed. This makes it possible to assess if the organization is achieving its goals on time. The plan must also create provisions for evaluating progress, as a plan without an evaluation mechanism is not so useful.

Finally, the organization must have a way to act upon the findings of its evaluation. These actions must lead to reduced environmental impact otherwise the organization cannot achieve full points during the assessment.

CATEGORY: ENVIRONMENT

Indicator 7: Does the organization maintain a monitoring system, measuring the significant environmental impacts?

'Measuring and monitoring' systems is a way to determine how much of a resource, be it energy, water or paper, an organization is using and the impact this use is having on the environment. This Guide is different from an action plan in that it is geared toward measuring specific elements within the action plan. The system is necessary for the action plan to be carried out but is not enough in and of itself to drive change.

To have such systems in place is important as they ensure that processes are operated in a standardized way regardless of who is undertaking them. If designed well, systems also create a clear process that people can follow to either obtain information or complete a task efficiently.

Potential sources of information

Utility bills, licensing details, certificates from external parties processing the organization's waste, government evaluations and reports.

Practical tips

It might be that some monitoring measures are mandatory to comply with national laws. In this case the assessor should be cautious as good CSR practice should go beyond minimal legal requirements.

This indicator focuses upon carbon emissions. However, climate change mitigation is of high importance for any kind of organization despite its size and the sector it works in.

Organizations are advised to set measurable and realistic goals. For instance, to reduce CO_2 emissions year on year. Quarterly targets that can be measured and monitored are helpful to track progress. A key performance indicator should then be established. For example, electricity consumption, the measurement of which would be recording the kilowatts of electricity used each month.

Methodology

1. Ensure that a person or department within the organization compiles and maintains utility bills and information on environmental impacts.
2. Organize this information so that it can be compared annually.
3. Undertake an annual assessment of whether the documentation is reflecting progress or not on environmental indicators linked to significant environmental impacts. These could include carbon emissions, water use, energy use, air emissions, amount of waste disposed of to landfill and any other environmental information relevant to the individual organization.

Scoring

Total score available: 4 pts; Yes = 4 pts; No = 0 pts

The emphasis in this part of the Assessment is to ensure that a system exists to evaluate the significance of an organization's use of materials and the subsequent and significant environmental impacts of such consumption. The organization will get points if a system exists and no points if there is no system.

Indicator 8: Does the organization have a training programme to help employees implement its environmental policy and action plan?

'Training programme' means a way of equipping employees with the knowledge and skills to act on their environmental responsibilities. This programme should be carried out on a regular basis, both to reflect changes in priorities and to keep employees' skills up to date.

It is good if there is a policy and action plan, but if employees do not know how to implement these strategies, beneficial CSR practice will not occur. Therefore, this indicator is designed to ensure that CSR happens in practice, not just in theory.

Potential sources of information

Training documents pertaining to CSR and notes from meetings with workers about the development of CSR training, training schedules and training policies.

Practical tips

The content and length of the training can be diverse among organizations. In some places it is a short, general introduction to environmental issues, whilst in others it is an extended, comprehensive exercise. This will depend on sector the organization operates in and its impacts. Regardless of the organization size and sector, making staff aware of global environmental problems and their personal and professional impact upon local, sustainable production and consumption, green procurement and production, and sustainable product life cycle issues is necessary to fulfill the principles of a responsible business.

The format of the training needs to be suited to the type of training content plus the audience type and location. For example, online training may be appropriate for geographically spread homeworking staff, whilst hands-on, 'toolbox talks' may be better for factory shop-floor workers.

CATEGORY: ENVIRONMENT

Methodology

1. Have senior staff develop training that is consistent with international CSR standards and the organization's own CSR policy.
2. Include staff input into training content to help improve the training.
3. Ensure that appropriate training format and content is developed and provided for each job category.

Scoring

Total score available: 4 pts; The organization has a training programme that it gives annually, as well as to new hires and all attendees have signed attendance sheets for the training = 4 pts; The organization has a documented training programme = 2 pts; The organization has no training programme = 0 pts

This type of training should happen on at least an annual basis, but preferably more often. The organization can receive full points under this indicator if can both conducts the training and document its occurrence. Such training can be a part of broader CSR training, but there must be at least a specific component focused upon the environment.

The training must be specific enough that staff will know how to encompass the elements of the action plan in their own job roles and responsibilities.

Indicator 9: Can the organization show a quantifiable reduction in annual carbon emissions?

'Quantifiable reduction' means a numeric drop in the amount of carbon emissions generated by an organization.

While it is important to have policies, strategies and action plans, and to act, the true test of an action is if it works. This indicator is therefore geared towards demonstrating that the action an organization is taking to reduce its environmental impact is really working.

Potential sources of information

Documents proving that steps are being taken to manage carbon emissions, e.g. an annual series of energy bills showing a reduction in energy use, records on energy consumption showing a lowering use of fossil fuel-based energy sources and a higher use of renewable energy.

Practical tips

Most organizations are taking measures to address climate change by managing energy consumption and looking for more energy efficient ways to cut their greenhouse gas emissions. However, the organizations should be interested in a real reduction (per product or revenue unit), not in lowering emissions resulting only from the drop of output. Renewable energy should be considered whenever possible.

The organization should first address emissions that come because of its internal operations, such as office work and in-house production facilities. Once these have been satisfactorily addressed and minimized goals can be extended to the reduction of carbon emissions caused by off-site operations. For example, carpooling and office waste reduction, recycling and reuse measures.

Methodology

1. Compile relevant energy, water, packaging and emissions bills and statistics.

2. Arrange the data into a form that shows comparative information year on year.

3. Use proper annual comparisons to show annual changes in environmental impact. For example, electricity use normalized using degree day data can make for a useful assessment of electricity used for space heating or cooling. Using a key performance indicator such as electricity used per degree day enables the effects of changes in weather to be negated whilst enabling the evaluation of space heating energy efficiency measures.

Scoring

Total score available: 4 pts; The organization can show a quantifiable reduction in its environmental impact based on a rolling 3-year average = 4 pts; The organization can show no increase in its environmental impact based on a rolling 3-year average = 2 pts; The organization cannot demonstrate either a reduction or no increase in its environmental impact based on a rolling 3-year average = 0 pts

Clearly, the bigger the reduction that can be shown the better. However, the focus initially can be getting emission levels falling. Although reductions are accepted both in absolute and normalized terms, it is a requirement that the lower level reflects a genuine drop in the carbon intensity, i.e. a drop caused by other business factors such as a fall in output will not do.

Indicator 10: Does the organization have a recycling programme?

A 'recycling programme' means not just segregation of recyclable materials but that those recyclable materials must be given to a specialised organization that undertakes recycling.

Recycling means not disposing of a product but treating it so that it can be re-used in some form in the future. It pertains to several different processes, including paper, plastic, water and batteries.

Relevance

Recycling is an important way to reduce environmental impact.

Potential sources of information

Recycling bins or areas, contracts with well-regarded recycling organizations.

Practical tips

If the organization collects waste and uses it for energy generation then this is a more responsible way of waste handling than just dumping the waste in landfill. However, the term recycling is about reuse of a waste rather than its incineration.

Of course, the organization's choice depends on availability of credible recycling organizations. However, this should not hinder the organization from developing innovative solutions and aim for 'zero waste' production processes.

Methodology

1. Identify what can and what cannot be recycled and an area to store recyclable materials.
2. Identify a contract with a credible recycling organization.

Scoring

Total score available: 4 pts; The organization collects recyclable materials and hands it over to a specialised, credible organization for recycling = 4 pts; The organization collects recyclable materials and leaves it for collection by an unknown party = 2 pts; The organization makes no effort to recycle = 0 pts

In order to receive points for this indicator, an organization must demonstrate that it undertakes recycling and does not just collect recyclable materials for later disposal by standard waste disposal methods.

Labor Relations

The relationship between the managers of the organization and their employees is the focus of the 5 indicators within this category. More specifically, labor relations encompass the business systems that tie employers and employees, management and unions allowing decisions to be made. Such decisions are significant as they cover areas such as wages, working conditions, hours of work, safety at work, security and grievances.

CATEGORY: LABOR RELARIONS

Indicator 11: Does the organization have a regularly evaluated action plan regarding labor and human resources?

A labor and human resources action plan should have established goals and associated improvement targets. These should then be developed into an action plan. Staff should understand the plan and be clear about their responsibilities for successfully addressing each action and the priority of those actions. A schedule for completing each action should be available, as well as how progress along the schedule is monitored, evaluated and communicated throughout the organization.

The action plan should be inclusive of the following types of work practices and areas, i.e.:

- Fair engagement with employee representatives
- Assurance of non-discrimination and gender equality
- Health and safety preventive actions
- Mitigation of job losses
- Establishment of remuneration levels and how people can earn more
- Establishment of fair conditions of work, beyond what is legally required
- Benefits in addition to those stipulated by law provided to workers of all contract types. For example, full-time, part-time, contract and seasonal.
- Grievance procedures and disciplinary action

This indicator is geared towards ensuring that organizations collect information regarding their social obligations and effectively, and in a timely way, act upon them.

If an organization has documented its performance, this means it is not just acting in some way on its social commitments, but also monitoring its actions.

CATEGORY: LABOR RELATIONS

Potential sources of information

An action plan covering labor issues and human resources issues that goes beyond minimum legal requirements.

Practical tips

Generally, organizations have documents such as Human Resources and Health and Safety polices and Codes of Conduct relevant to this indicator.

In most EU countries this may seem an easy indicator as the labour relations are well reflected in European legal systems. However, attention should be paid to such issues as bullying prevention, and gender and other equal opportunities that may not be fully covered by legal frameworks.

Methodology

1. Incorporate inputs from senior management and employees in determining whether the plan covers the needs of employees.

2. Designate a senior staff member to oversee the collection and review of data and report findings on a regular basis to all employees.

3. Based on the findings of the review, decide on ways to implement the labor and human resources programme more effectively.

Scoring

Total score available: 4 pts; The organization has an action plan and evaluates its progress based on the plan = 4 pts; The organization has an action plan = 2 pts; The organization has no action plan = 0 pts

This plan must cover labor and human rights practices that go beyond the law. In order to receive full points under this indicator, the organization must not only have an action plan but must evaluate the plan.

Indicator 12: Do employees have official representation in the organization?

'Representation' means that employees are taken notice of at senior level by any of the following means: trade unions, employee council, input into their terms and conditions of work, regular documented feedback session or some other formal feedback process.

Employee representation is a multi-stakeholder approach to negotiating working conditions. The over-arching idea of this indicator is that it is a proxy for the power balance between employers and employees and for the level of stakeholder engagement whilst setting workplace conditions.

This process takes place differently in different countries, and different laws facilitate or obstruct its practice in different ways.

Employee engagement should happen in all organizations as getting employees involved in the way their workplace operates can be helpful in organizations of all sizes.

Potential sources of information

Collective bargaining agreements, trade union membership, existence of an employee council, any evidence of employee comments being included in terms of work.

Practical tips

Management philosophy suggests that even if a 'bottom up' initiative does not exist it is worth having official representation. In such a scenario a group of employees should be formed that would have regular meetings with senior managers in order to discuss questions, feedback and other employee requests.

Methodology

1. Identify a group or body that represents the interests of staff in the organization.
2. Identify a process for regularly engaging with this group or body.

3. Present evidence of at least one instance in which input from this body, or directly from staff, has been included in the organization's operations.

Scoring

Total score available: 4 pts; There are trade union meetings, employment council meetings or other type of employee representation in the organization = 4 pts; There is no official employee representation in the organization = 0 pts

Employees must be given a voice at management level. Management cannot merely accept input from employees and then do nothing about it but must incorporate it into the way the organization operates. In order to receive full points under this indicator, the organization must show evidence of employee feedback and how such views are being considered.

Indicator 13: Does the organization have a health and safety system?

'Processes to prevent' means that an organization has regularly evaluated the health and safety issues required by law. These reviews then help staff determine areas in which they can implement systems to further reduce future problems from occurring.

In order to prevent fatal accidents, it is important for an organization to assess the conditions and frequency of accidents so that the organization can learn from things that go wrong, pick up on trends and rectify problems before they cause serious or fatal injuries.

Potential sources of information

Accident and injury logs, accident and injury template, completed accident and injury forms, documented safety processes, sign in sheets from health and safety training.

Practical tips

All organizations are legally obligated to regularly train staff on health and safety issues. Lack of valid training means serious sanctions for employers. In some cases, preventive measures in addition to those prescribed by law, might be put in place. For example, to prevent repetitive strain injuries an organization may provide employees subsidized membership of fitness centers and swimming pools, as well as paid-for preventive medical checks.

Methodology

1. Demonstrate a written process to prevent health and safety issues.

2. Demonstrate health and safety training materials.

3. Provide additional training documents covering concerns arising from injury and accident records.

CATEGORY: LABOR RELATIONS

Scoring

Total score available: 4 pts; The organization has processes to prevent recurring accidents and injuries = 4 pts; The organization trains its staff on H&S issues on a regular basis = 2 pts; The organization has inadequate, or no health and safety processes or training = 0 pts

This indicator goes beyond the law to assess whether organizations use information to make improvements and to put in place preventative H&S measures. Both training and a process for injury prevention are important components of this indicator. Both must be in place for an organization to receive full points.

Indicator 14: Does the organization have plans to mitigate the adverse impacts of job reductions?

'Mitigate adverse impacts' means taking steps to alleviate the burden on people when job losses occur. This indicator does not suggest that organizations should go bankrupt trying to help staff they have to let go. It merely recognizes that there are actions an organization can take, beyond those prescribed in law that can help reduce the difficulty workers face when they lose their jobs.

Part of an organization's responsibility as an employer is to plan and manage staff turnover, including redundancy or job reductions. While there are usually laws in this area, organizations can also undertake activities such as re-training and helping staff they must let go to find work elsewhere.

Potential sources of information

Financial statements, overhead costs, any justifications for dismissing staff and payroll records.

Practical tips

This indicator is especially relevant in a situation when the economy is shrinking and can be viewed as a positive risk management measure.

The necessity to have a plan of action during job reductions might be confirmed to be legally mandatory. In such a case the organization should also analyze activities it does, or could do, that are not covered by law.

Methodology

1. Work with government officials and staff to establish fair terms of dismissal, programmes and techniques for ensuring that the burden on dismissed staff and their families is minimized.

2. Identify a written document outlining plans in the event of job reductions.

3. Evaluate the plans to see if they go beyond legal compliance in providing support for employees who lose their jobs.

4. Determine if the plans incorporate job retraining, helping staff find new, or alternative solutions to keep staff employed in times of economic downturn.

Scoring

Total score available: 4 pts; The organization helps staff to find new job = 1 pt; The organization uses alternative solutions to keep staff employed = 1 pt; The organization provides severance pay above legal requirements = 1 pts; The organization provides job re-training = 1 pts

The organization must show it has taken steps beyond those prescribed in law to assist employees if job losses occur. The actions that are geared towards keeping staff in jobs receive higher scores than efforts merely meant to bridge the gap between employment.

Indicator 15: Does the organization have an effective grievance procedure?

A 'grievance procedure' means a process by which employees can make their concerns and complaints known to the organization. It can take different forms. These include a suggestion box scheme, a formal process run by human resources or a 'whistleblowing' hotline provided by a third-party organization.

Staff need the opportunity to air concerns and complaints about their employers. Without an effective grievance process, an organization can experience workers unrest, dissatisfaction amongst its workforce, a loss of productivity and other undesirable impacts on the workplace environment. This can sometimes be tricky for small organizations as it is easier to make anonymous complaints in a larger organization. However, counterbalancing that in small organisations, staff disturbances potentially have a larger impact as each personal within the organization is more prominent.

Potential sources of information

Documented grievance procedure, grievance procedure content, notes or minutes from grievance procedure meetings and training, signed staff attendance sheets, examples of grievances submitted, examples of resolutions achieved through the grievance procedure.

Practical tips

The effectiveness of a grievance procedure might be misunderstood. So, to help, 'an effective grievance procedure' is when there is no whistleblowing, negative feedback and only grievance cases via the official channels. However, it might also be that if there is no trust in the grievance system then staff are unlikely to use it.

Methodology

1. Meet with senior staff to develop a grievance procedure compliant with legal standards and best practice guidelines.

2. Consult staff on the content and delivery of the grievance procedure training.

3. Develop grievance procedure training to ensure that all staff know and understand how to use the proper channels of reporting grievances in order to achieve a satisfactory resolution to the grievance.

Scoring

Total score available: 4 pts; The organization treats grievances anonymously and the grievances are dealt externally or by human resources = 4 pts; The organization deals with grievances internally and does not do so anonymously = 2 pts; The organization does not have a grievance procedure = 0 pts

The organization must offer a way for employees to voice their concerns anonymously and to have them addressed. It is not enough to get points for this indicator if the organization does not process and address the grievances. Organizations also get higher points for anonymous systems as this element is critical for an effective process.

Community Relations

The links and interactions between the organization and the groups of people in which it operates is what the next category of 5 indicators probes.

Good relations offer positive opportunities for a mutually beneficial relationship with the communities in which organizations operate. Such communities include the local neighbourhood, specialist communities of interest as well as far-off groups of people supplying raw materials. The ways in which community relations are managed can help, or hinder, the organization in achieving its overall mission.

Indicator 16: Does the organization have a community engagement action plan?

A 'community engagement action plan' means a plan that includes:

- Goals and associated improvement targets
- Prioritized and time-limited actions necessary for meeting such targets
- Clearly identified staff responsibilities for each action
- Monitoring and evaluation processes for each action
- Ways to communicate progress of the action plan

Such a community engagement action plan should consider the following aspects of its operations and how it effectively engages with:

- Stakeholders
- CSR industry groups
- Volunteering schemes
- Apprenticeship schemes
- The local community especially prior to acquiring property or starting new business operations
- Affected communities about potential emergencies

A part of the organization's social responsibility is to act as a good corporate citizen. In other words, an organization has a responsibility toward the communities in which it operates. To meet this responsibility, it must therefore firstly establish a plan for community engagement.

Potential sources of information

Documented community engagement process, notes or minutes from meetings with community stakeholders, action plans for resolving any disputes and reflecting constructive guidelines for engagement.

Practical tips

Community engagement is one of the strongest assets of organizations that are engaged in CSR. Such community engagement comprises formal and informal ways of staying connected to the stakeholders who have an actual or potential interest in, or effect upon, the organization.

Methodology

1. Meet with senior staff and community stakeholders to determine a community engagement plan.

2. Determine indicators for all key stakeholders in establishing an equitable, mutually beneficial means of engaging in future projects and interactions.

3. Based on the results of these discussions, determine a system for the organization to use in engaging with communities on material issues, including when to invoke the plan, which staff are responsible for the engagement and how to resolve disputes.

Scoring

Total score available: 4 pts; The organization has an action plan and regularly evaluates its progress = 4 pts; The organization has an action plan but does not regularly review its progress = 2 pts; The organization has no action plan = 0 pts

This indicator is based on the goal to develop trust and communication between the organization and community. Organizations will not get points merely for having an action plan. They must show that they evaluate the plan in a meaningful way that adequately accounts for the needs of the community in organizational decision-making.

Indicator 17: Does the organization engage in regular dialogue with its key stakeholders?

Prioritizing stakeholders

You may have a long list of people and organizations who are stakeholders within your organization. Some of these may have the power either to block or to advance your environmental work. Some may be interested in what you are doing whilst others may not care. Categorise the stakeholders identifying their power over, and interest in, the environmental performance of the organisation. Using the four categories of high and low power, and high and low interest the relative positions of the stakeholders can then be placed in a matrix in which the horizontal axis is labelled interest (from low on the left, to high on the right) and the vertical axis labelled from low power at the bottom to high power at the top – see Figure 1. By doing this the ways to engage with these stakeholders becomes clearer as you need to manage closely those with both high power and high interest. These are the people you must fully engage with and make the greatest efforts to satisfy.

For those with high power and low interest you need to communicate sufficiently with these people to keep them satisfied but not so much that they become bored with your message. You should keep those with low power and high interest adequately informed and talk to them to ensure that no major issues are arising as these people can often be helpful with the detail of your environmental work. Whilst those with low power and low interest should be monitored, but not bored with excessive communication.

Stakeholder groups can include for example, government, charities, trade unions, community-based organizations and investors.

'Regular dialogue' means consulting key stakeholders at least when the organization takes a decision that impacts them. It also means communicating regularly on the organization's CSR commitments, e.g. releasing a CSR report or putting details of CSR practices on the organization's website.

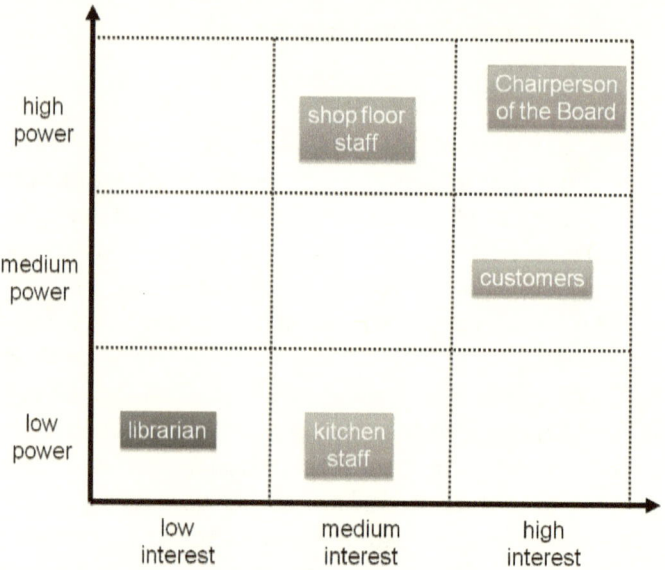

Figure 1 Power and Interest Stakeholder Matrix

Transparency is a cornerstone of good CSR practice. Regular dialogue with key stakeholders is important to ensure the long term 'license to operate' and may reduce or prevent problems with these people in the future. The challenges set by stakeholders may even feed positively into the development of new products or systems.

Potential sources of information

Notes and minutes from meetings with community stakeholders pertaining to the organization's property acquisitions, any agreements reached, problems or remediation plans determined as a result of the engagement process, annual reports, websites.

Practical tips

Organizations undertaking CSR initiatives must be ready to communicate externally what they have realized and what they still hope to achieve. It is the organization that must define its key stakeholders. Depending on the issue, the size of the organization and other factors, organizations will also define what 'regular dialogue' means to them.

In most organizations dialogue is usually taking place, but it is not always at the same level in relation to different key stakeholders, i.e. it may be regular and formal with employees, but much less regular with vendors. It may result since dialogue is 'undeveloped', or from a rational point of view some stakeholders are less important for the organization. For example, engagement might already exist under the auspices of the current management approach that an organization is currently conducting, such as ISO 9000 or ISO 14000.

Methodology

1. Identify and prioritize key stakeholders.
2. Determine how often and under what conditions to engage a dialogue.
3. Establish terms for how and when to incorporate community feedback into the organization's decision-making process.

Scoring

Total score available: 4 pts; The organization initiates regular engagement with stakeholders = 4 pts; The organization engages with stakeholders when stakeholders approach the organization with specific concerns they have about its operations = 3 pts; The organization communicates its CSR performance on a regular basis = 2 pts; The organization does not engage with stakeholders = 0 pts

CSR communication can take on a range of formats, e.g. public talks and presentations, newsletters, reports, online reporting and via the organization's products and packaging. The communication should provide information on current CSR performance and future ambitions.

One-way communication with stakeholders is not enough, though. The engagement must be meaningful as both sides should acknowledge and operate in recognition of the other's point of view and needs. Organizations will get extra points for initiating an engagement with stakeholders to head off any adverse effects of the organization's practices.

Indicator 18: Does the organization actively participate in CSR associations and forums or engage with any local charities?

Definition

'CSR associations and forums' means industry groups such as the Electronics Industry Code of Conduct, CSR forums, such as Business in the Community or local branches of the UN Global Compact, or similar initiatives.

'Engagement with local charities' means working with local charities to ensure a mutually-beneficial community development agenda.

Participation in CSR associations and forums is a good way for organizations to stay in touch with their social obligations. This occurs both in terms of receiving feedback and using other members as a resource for creative and innovation solutions to social and environmental challenges.

If SMEs can participate in these groups, it can be helpful to get ideas for their businesses, but the resource constraints might prevent them from doing so. However, they can still engage with local NGOs even if they cannot participate in CSR associations or forums.

'Description' + *'relevance'* goes here but without sub-heading

Potential sources of information

Receipts from payments to forums or associations, evidence of participation in initiatives and pilot projects run by relevant organizations.

Practical tips

This indicator should analyze if the organization actively participates in CSR associations, forums or initiatives of local charities that foster specific CSR values such as environmental education.

CATEGORY: COMMUNITY RELATIONS

Methodology

1. Meet with senior staff to determine whether the CSR issues facing the organization could best be met by CSR associations and forums.

2. Participate in associations and forums that would contribute to the effective implementation of the organization's CSR programme.

Scoring

Total score available: 4 pts; The organization participates in the activities of a CSR- related organization or local charity between 2 and 5 times a year = 4 pts; The organization is a member of a CSR-related organization or local charity but is not active in this group = 2 pts; The organization does not engage with CSR-related organizations or local charities = 0 pts

It is not enough for organizations to be members of such forums to receive full points for this indicator: They must show active participation, such as regularly contributing to such initiatives.

Indicator 19: Does the organization offer volunteering time, invest in or support any local community initiatives?

Community investment can happen as a core part of the business. It can also occur as a positive consequence of the organization's activities even though it is not an essential part of the organization's operations. Some examples of community investment include:

- pro-bono support
- partnerships with educational institutions
- supporting research
- training, skill and capacity building
- legal, management and consultancy work
- In-kind donations

This indicator is also geared toward establishing a sense of trust between the organization and the community. It enables employees to develop extra skills that they can bring back to the organization.

Potential sources of information

Documentation about relevant partnerships with community organizations, including project plans, minutes or notes from meetings, communications between parties, formal agreements between parties, financial or material support, documentation about the relevant partnership, including project plans, minutes or notes from meetings, communications between relevant parties.

Practical tips

The distinction of core and non-core business refers to the way and the type volunteering occurs. Core business means the fundamental activities of the organization, and so volunteering in this case is closely connected with this activity and staff capabilities stemming from this activity. An example is where employees give pro bono professional services to clients from marginalized community groups, seeking to activate social inclusion and promote entrepreneurship of persons with disabilities.

Non-core business volunteering happens when the work provided is not related in any aspect to the fundamental activity of the organization. For example, employees of a consultancy firm painting the walls of a school.

Methodology

1. Identify organization policies on volunteering in the community.

2. Identify any volunteering agreements or public commitments to volunteer.

3. Appropriately publicize the volunteering experience.

Scoring

Total score available: 4 pts; The organization invests in the community in a way that reflects its core business activity = 4 pts; The organization invests in the community in a way that reflects non-core business activity = 2 pts; The organization makes no community investments = 0 pts

Innovative, carefully designed and developed, targeted activities qualify as core business activities, so an organization would gain points here if it could link the support to its own initiatives in terms of driving innovation in its products and services.

Non-core business activity would qualify for points if it contributes to the community. For example, building a park or holding a fair to raise money for a good cause.

Indicator 20: Does the organization offer training schemes to facilitate skills development?

'Training' means a fixed-term position within an organization in order to foster skills development for the trainee. Programmes can last from a couple of weeks to a couple of years and could be in the form of an apprenticeship or internship.

This indicator is good both from the perspective of developing a sense of trust and appreciation within the community with respect to promoting positive social development. Good training schemes can contribute to skills development within communities. By deploying such schemes organizations can benefit from operating in a more stable business environment and have a bigger pool of people from which to recruit.

Potential sources of information

Documented policy on engaging trainees or interns, apprenticeship or other trainee and intern contracts.

Practical tips

Some organizations offer apprenticeships for students from local universities, colleges or secondary schools. Most of them have students in organizations to learn new skills although different organizations approach this activity differently. For example, some employ students simply as part-time employees, whilst others have Graduate Trainee Programs.

Methodology

1. Meet with senior staff to determine whether the organization would benefit from and would be able to contribute to a training program consistent with legal standards of employing trainees.

2. If so, develop a scheme that optimizes the trainee's value to the organization's operations whilst also considering the trainee's skills development opportunities.

3. Have the trainee(s) complete an evaluation form at the end of the training program to determine whether the program is mutually beneficial and how it could be improved.

Scoring

Total score available: 4 pts; The organization offers a paid training scheme that enables trainees to come out with a certification of their skill level = 4 pts; The organization offers an unpaid training scheme that provides for skills development but no certification = 2 pts; The organization does not offer a training scheme = 0 pts

The key is whether the scheme equips trainees with new skills that can secure employment in the future. An organization would not gain many points here for taking on a student for 2 weeks whose sole job was to make coffee, instead of also getting to learn some more substantive office skills.

Business Environment

The last 5 indicators are designed to investigate the business environment in which the organization operates. 'Business environment' is a term that includes all the factors that affect the organization's business activities. These can come from within the organization itself and can come from outside the organization. Such internal factors can include the relationship between the managers and their employees, whilst external issues are like how the organization deals with issues in its supply chain, different national laws and pan-global protocols.

Indicator 21: Does the organization assess the human rights, health and safety, anti-corruption and environmental practices of its supply chain?

'Assess supply chain' means checking to see if suppliers are upholding adequate social and environmental standards, in compliance with the law, international standards and best CSR practice. Some organizations have robust social auditing programmes for which they hire external social auditing organizations to assess their suppliers. Other organizations meanwhile may only issue self-assessments to suppliers to do a cursory evaluation of the labor standards at the supplying facility.

Supply chain concerns have become prominent in recent years and particularly for larger organizations that outsource their goods and services. This can be a reputational risk and increasingly can be a legal concern in some contexts. It is therefore important for organizations to understand the risk to their businesses from contracting parties who do not uphold adequate CSR practices.

Potential sources of information

Documented policy on engagement with supply chain business partners or codes of conduct for suppliers, assessment tools reflecting analysis of underlying causes of violations, metrics on human rights and anti-corruption practices at business partners, corrective action plans, evidence of remediation, evidence of using relevant information to inform improved supply chain management policy and sourcing contracts.

Practical tips

Supply chain assessment, for example, might already exist under the auspices of the current management approach that an organization is already conducting, such as ISO 9000, ISO 14000 or Forest Stewardship Council certification.

Due to the complexity of international supply chains and the corresponding CSR issues which can arise, this indicator might be thought of as too difficult. To help with this, organizations could use existing tools for the assessment of contractors were possible.

How import supply chain issues are to the organization can be indicated by the number of suppliers which the organization has refused to work with. For instance, contracts might be terminated due to:

- embezzlement
- accidents that have happened within the supplier's business
- refusal of work in line with the organization's Code of Conduct

Methodology

1. Meet with relevant staff to determine the risk of human rights abuses and corruption in the supply chain and/or among business partners.

2. If there is deemed to be a risk, determine the most efficient way of assessing human rights and corruption practices within the business partners. That could be via social and environmental audits, participation in industry groups on labor and environmental practices, or via a regional risk assessment.

3. Determine the best way to reduce the risk given the organization's resources, size and feedback from supplier and contractor assessments.

4. Determine at which point to engage with suppliers to help improve their social and environmental practices and at which point to either cut the contract or refuse to engage in a contract based on poor social and environmental practices.

Scoring

Total score available: 4 pts; The organization assesses its supply chain and makes sourcing decisions based on the assessments, including engaging with non-compliant suppliers to support improvement of their ethical standards = 4 pts; The organization conducts assessments of only its first tier suppliers = 2 pts; The organization conducts no assessments of its suppliers = 0 pts

CATEGORY: BUSINESS ENVIRONMENT

The organization can get points for this indicator for a mere assessment of first tier suppliers. To gain additional points organizations need to show that they monitor the entire supply chain, work with suppliers to improve standards and make sourcing decisions based on thorough evaluations of their suppliers' social and environmental practices.

CATEGORY: BUSINESS ENVIRONMENT

Indicator 22: Does the organization engage in sustainable procurement?

'Sustainable procurement practices' means making decisions on where to source goods and services based on the environmental, social and long-term performance of the supplier. For example, using Forest Stewardship Council certified timber or organic produce.

This indicator is particularly important as a means of embedding sustainable business practices in the way an organization operates.

Potential sources of information

Sustainable procurement policy, sourcing contracts that include sustainable requirements.

Practical tips

Be wary of 'green washing' – those organizations that 'talk' a lot about how sustainable they are, but when investigated lack substantial actions in this business area.

Organizations may consider the sustainability of the materials and chemicals they use in their products and services. Such assessment should look beyond the organization's 'gates' and into the operations of their suppliers in an ongoing effort to reduce costs and risk.

Organizations might use substantial sustainability-assessment tools like life-cycle assessment. Others meanwhile might take a lesser stance and rely upon information provided by their suppliers to identify the materials in their products that may pose significant environmental, health and safety risks.

Methodology

1. Identify a sustainable procurement policy that acknowledges the legal standard and exceeds minimal legal requirements.

2. Identify sourcing contracts with sustainable procurement requirements.

3. Identify an organizational practice of favoring suppliers with strong sustainability credentials.

Scoring

Total score available: 4 pts; The organization makes sourcing decisions based on sustainable practices of all suppliers in the supply chain, including engaging with non-compliant suppliers to support improvement of their environmental standards = 4 pts; The organization tries to incorporate sustainable considerations into its procurement practices where possible = 2 pts; The organization undertakes no sustainable procurement = 0 pts

Some countries have legal requirements surrounding sustainable procurement as a result of EU law. In order to get full points for this indicator, the organization will have to show that it has gone beyond such minimal legal requirements in making truly sustainable business decisions.

Indicator 23: Does the organization have anti-bribery and corruption procedures?

'Anti-bribery and corruption procedures' means being able to determine whether an incident should be considered bribery or corruption and then being able to take steps to stop the illegal or unethical act.

This is an example of where there are often laws, but the laws sometimes do not get fully enforced. It can be difficult for organizations to behave ethically where the larger business environment does not encourage good business ethics. It is therefore critical for organizations to have plans and courses of action to address corrupt practices.

Potential sources of information

Anti-corruption policy, signed statements from staff stating that they understand the policy and promise to uphold anti-corruption standards established in the policy.

Practical tips

Corruption is the abuse of entrusted power for private gain. This means both financial gain and other, nonfinancial advantages. Bribery and corruption mean different things for small and large organizations. In small organizations it might be understood as private work of the employees. For example, a carpenter channels clients' orders to her own workshop diverting it from the organization to her private business.

Large organizations might have anti-bribery and anti-corruption policies included in their Codes of Conduct or even special rules regarding gifts. It might be an external person appointed to deal with supplier/client complaints in case of possible bribery or corruption.

Methodology

1. Meet with senior staff to determine the areas of the business susceptible to corrupt practices

2. Develop an anti-corruption policy based on accepted international standards, such as the OECD Guidelines

3. Consult with employees on the content of the policy and the most effective way to convey the policy and implement its standards in the workplace

Scoring

Total score available: 4 pts; The organization has rules and procedures to analyse and counter bribery and corruption practices = 4 pts; The organization has no rules and procedures to analyse and counter bribery and corruption practices = 0 pts

An organization will get points here for having a strategy addressing this indicator. To get full points organizations must demonstrate transparency in its behavior and a commitment to ensuring a business environment in which bribery and corruption are both unacceptable and actively discouraged.

Indicator 24: Does the organization have a policy and procedure for making its lobbying efforts transparent?

Lobbying is standard practice in politics and can be done legally and ethically. However, it is quite easy to cross the line into unethical lobbying. Therefore, for this indicator, 'making lobbying efforts transparent' means that an organization should disclose the amount of money and resources it spends in trying to promote its agenda on the political stage.

This indicator relates to the above bribery and corruption indicators. This is because when organizations lobby politicians or powerful organization, they are exerting influence for policy decisions in their favor, potentially without consideration of less powerful stakeholders. In order to counteract undue power and influence, organizations should disclose their lobbying practices to make themselves accountable to society and other stakeholders, and in order not to wield excessive power.

Potential sources of information

Documented lobbying policy, including content on disclosure of lobbying practices and the resources spent on it, annual report or CSR report with lobbying disclosure information.

Practical tips

In some countries 'lobbying' might have a sense of something unethical, which is seen as close to corruption and means something which has nothing in common with transparency. One important step in making lobbying more transparent is to instead enroll in an industry interest group, such as an official association. Such a group will then lobby on behalf of the organization.

Methodology

1. Meet with senior staff to determine whether the organization should engage with political entities.

2. If it is determined to be beneficial to do so, develop a policy that ensures engagement in an ethical, transparent way. For example publish statements on levels of contributions and the means of interacting with political entities.

Scoring

Total score available: 4 pts; The organization has a policy and procedure for making its lobbying efforts transparent = 4 pts; The organization has no policy and procedure for making its lobbying efforts transparent = 0 pts

Given that there is often a fine line between ethical and unethical practices for this indicator, the emphasis is on transparency. For the organization to have a policy stating that it lobbies according to the law or ethically will not be good enough for full points. It needs to produce clear evidence that it fully discloses its lobbying efforts, preferably with evidence of this disclosure.

Indicator 25: Does the organization train its staff on ethical supply chain measures and anti-bribery and anti-corruption measures?

Training in this context means educating employees on how to perform their jobs in an ethical way. For instance, educating buyers on how to engage with suppliers in a way that conveys the organization's standard of adhering to ethical business practices in sourcing its goods and services. Another example is training employees on how to uphold the organization's code of practice, including when it is acceptable to receive gifts, and other standards of ethical conduct.

It is important for organizations to have a plan and policy in this area. However, in order to put these tools into action, employees must know how to do their part.

Potential sources of information

Documentation of anti-corruption training, including training content, attendance lists with attendee signatures.

Practical tips

Most organizations have a Code of Conduct that is presented to all new hires. In this way every employee is informed about anti-corruption and anti-bribery measures. Also, information might come via the organization's website, internal communications and e-learning. Ethical supply chain measures are mainly presented to procurement departments.

Methodology

1. Meet with senior staff to determine the content of the ethical supply chain and anti-corruption training.
2. Consult with employees on necessary components of the training.
3. Administer training at regular intervals, requiring a signed attendance at training sessions.

4. Collect feedback from staff attending the sessions to assess comprehension of the policy and how to implement it, as well as how to improve the training.

Scoring

Total score available: 4 pts; The organization has a training program that it gives annually, as well as to new hires, and all attendees have signed attendance sheets for the trainings = 4 pts; The organization has a documented training program = 2 pts; The organization has no training programme in this area = 0 pts

To gain points for this indicator, organizations will need to show that they conduct training in these areas for all new employees, as well as regular training for existing staff.

Example Assessment-scoring Template

The template overleaf can be used by assessors as they carry-out the CSR Self-Assessment to record their findings. Specifically, for each of the five categories: the scores, remarks and suggested actions identified for each of the 25 indicators.

Category & Indicator	Score	Remarks	Suggested actions
Governance			
1			
2			
3			
4			
5			
Subtotal (20 max)			
Environment			
6			
7			
8			
9			
10			
Subtotal (20 max)			
Labor issues			
11			
12			
13			
14			
15			
Subtotal (20 max)			
Community Relations			
16			
17			
18			
19			
20			
Subtotal (20 max)			
Business Environment			
21			
22			
23			
24			
25			
Subtotal (20 max)			
TOTAL (100 max)			

www.ingramcontent.com/pod-product-compliance
Lightning Source LLC
Chambersburg PA
CBHW020606220526
45463CB00006B/2467